Faster Than a Speeding Bullet:
The Rise of the Graphic Novel

Faster Than a Speeding Bullet:
The Rise of the Graphic Novel

Stephen Weiner

NANTIER · BEALL · MINOUSTCHINE
Publishing inc.
new york

ISBN 978-1-56163-702-7

Library of Congress Control Number: 2012947465

Faster than a Speeding Bullet: The Rise of the Graphic Novel ©2003 Stephen Weiner

© 2012 Stephen Weiner for the second edition updates

Covers and artwork © their respective owners

Editor: N. C. Christopher Couch, except for updates

Foreword ©2003 Will Eisner

Cover art ©2003 Jeff Smith

Cover coloring by Steve Hamaker

Book Design by Chris Shadoian

For Ken, my brother
1949-2002
& for Bill Sleator
1945-2011

Contents

Foreword
Will Eisner

At the very moment in its history when the lowly comic book has at long last reached maturity it is important to have this excellent account of its journey from "literary fast food" to acceptable popular literature.

My applause for this work stems from my long and often frustrating involvement with comics as a medium. When I entered the profession—I was present at its birth—comic books, which were then called magazines, were dismissed as cheap entertainment for kids. They were disdained by the arbiters of our culture. I myself had only a visceral belief in the viability of the art or its future as acceptable literature. There was no evidence of its endurance as anything other than a fleeting fad of popular culture. History has proved otherwise.

At this writing almost seventy years later, comic book publishing thrives, providing opportunity for young creators and a body of popular literature firmly built on its own picture-story language. Available to readers now are a variety of categories from simple, thirty-two-page adventure, horror, superhero, instructional, reportage, and experimental comics and Japanese manga to the weighty graphic novels.

The manner of their creation has evolved from a work written and drawn by a single individual to a wedding between writer and artist. This has established a creative process that employs the skills of an accomplished writer and an artist of great sophistication. All of which has attracted critical approval and elevated the standards of the medium.

Superhero comics are mined by the motion picture industry for ideas, plots, and audiences. Motion picture adaptation of comics is now widespread.

Japanese manga, with their animation-related artwork, are finding a huge following among American teenage readers.

Meanwhile, establishment bookstores are assigning shelf space for Pulitzer Prize and other award winners as well as serious graphic novels that address adults.

The most significant evidence of comics' arrival, however, is their acceptance and acknowledgment by public librarians. The inclusion of graphic novels in their collections is a most welcome happening and, I might say, about time.

It was the converging of our interest in this awakening that provided me with an opportunity to exchange with Steve an observation of the current movement by the tectonic plates of our literary world and introduced me to this work. Steve Weiner has produced a very responsible survey and introduction to this literary phenomenon. Read it, learn, and enjoy.

Preface

In 1986, many working in the comics field thought that the breakthrough into mainstream culture they'd waited for was about to happen. That year, DC Comics released *Watchmen* and *Batman: The Dark Knight Returns,* both sophisticated superhero stories aimed at adult readers. Pantheon Books published *Maus,* a holocaust survival story which eventually earned a Pulitzer Prize.

The breakthrough the comics industry hoped for didn't happen in 1986, but that year was a turning point. From then on, cartoonists aimed higher and hoped more than ever that their books would break—or at least peek—out beyond the traditional comic book readership, and focused more on stories holding appeal to readers who didn't care for traditional comic books.

In 1996, I published a little guide for librarians, *100 Graphic Novels for Public Libraries.* As a result, I was asked to speak before interested groups at libraries and academic conferences about comics and graphic novels. The audiences for these talks were always curious about this field, so new to them, and I'd end each presentation with a question and answer period. After responding to a few questions about individual graphic novels, a member of the audience would inevitably ask, "How did this happen? How did the comics field grow to produce these things like *Maus,* things called graphic novels?" In 2001 NBM published my follow-up book, *The 101 Best Graphic Novels,* which reached out both to and beyond librarians with more information about the form. More talks followed, and I was asked the same, inevitable question even more frequently.

This book is my answer. It's informed by observing the comic book industry over a thirty-year period, the numerous histories of comics I've read, and interviews I've conducted with comic creators. Those whom I interviewed for this book are listed in the acknowledgments.

Graphic novels, as I define them, are book–length comic books that are meant to be read as one story. This broad term includes collections of stories in genres such as mystery, superhero, or supernatural, that are meant to be read apart from their corresponding ongoing comic book storyline; heart-rending works such as Art Spiegelman's *Maus;* and nonfiction pieces such as Joe Sacco's journalistic work, *Palestine.* As is the case with my other books, this book was written to learn more about a field I've enjoyed for most of my life.

Here, then, is how the comics industry grew up, took itself seriously, and made enough noise so that mainstream readers were finally forced to pay it serious attention.

ACKNOWLEDGMENTS

*For their help with this book, the author
would like to thank the following people:*

Steve Bissette
Peggy Burns
Chris Couch
Jim Crocker
Tony Davis
Tom Devlin
Tavish Donahue
Eric Drooker
Will Eisner
Jules Feiffer
Neil Gaiman
Craig Shaw Gardner
Lorraine Garland
Kathleen Glosan
Judy Hansen
Ben Katchor
Denis Kitchen
Peter Kuper
Scott McCloud
Terry Nantier
Richard Pini
Wendy Pini
Eric Reynolds
Chris Shadoian
Art Spiegelman
Chris Staros
Dan Vado

*Special thanks to Jeff Smith,
for telling me to write this book.*

I long for the mantle
of the great wanderers, who lighted
their steps by the lamp
of pure hunger and pure thirst,

And whichever way they lurched was the way

—Galway Kinnell, *The Book of Nightmares*

Like a vision she dances across
the porch as the radio plays.
—Bruce Springsteen

The First Comics
Americans Embrace a New Art Form

Americans had seen comics published before 1895, but Richard F. Outcault's single-panel cartoon, *The Yellow Kid,* was the first to catch widespread public attention. America was undergoing a cultural revolution. The movie industry was beginning, and tinkering with the product that would become radio had begun a few years earlier. Comics in the newspaper were another new form of entertainment, and the public embraced them. Soon products featuring the image of the Yellow Kid were everywhere: on shirts and cigars, lunch pails and cigarette cards, stationery and dolls.

Within a few short years, comic strips themselves were omnipresent, and not only because newspaper editors liked them. Publishers discovered that comic strips sold newspapers. Radios became widely available by the 1920s, but they were not a visual medium. Comic strips were a welcome relief in homes that otherwise had only novels as printed entertainment. Most of the comic strips published were forgettable, as with any medium, but some were terrific: E. C. Segar's *Popeye,* Al Capp's *Li'l Abner,* George Herriman's *Krazy Kat,* and Hal Foster's *Prince Valiant.* Comics appealed to readers

1

It'd happin agin an' agin fo' dek-aides: the romantic foibles of Al Capp's *Li'l Abner* (1935).

because they seemed easy to decode, and words were tacked on as dialogue to make the messages even clearer. Every picture told a story.

Comic books, magazines containing a few stories, were first published in the early 1930s, and were initially reprints of newspaper comic strips. But quickly comic book publishers realized that there was a market for new stories and sought out fresh material.

Early comic book magazines consisted of genre stories told in comic book format, including mysteries, adventure, and romance. To provide publishers with fresh stories for this burgeoning medium, companies sprang up, employing teams of artists and writers to create the stories as quickly and cheaply as possible. Completed stories were sold to comic book publishers such as DC and Timely (later Marvel).

The comic book world really exploded, however, when Jerry Siegel and Joe Shuster, a couple of Jewish kids from the Midwest, created Superman, ushering in a new tradition in heroic storytelling. Other superheroes followed Superman. Just as with comic strips, most of the new creations were mediocre, but some stood out—Batman, Wonder Woman, Captain America, Captain Marvel, and Plastic Man. Popeye, Little Orphan Annie and Li'l Abner found the doorway out of the comic strip into successful adaptations in other media, and many superheroes have become stars of film, plays, and novels.

During the Second World War, comic books featured decidedly patriotic heroes. Led by Captain America, who landed a roundhouse punch on Hitler's chin on the cover of his very first issue, these heroes had the war well underway before the country officially began fighting. Once the war began, many heroes, super and otherwise, spent a great deal of their energy fighting with the Allies. Stories were predictable, often crude and enthusiastic propaganda, and the craftsmanship of the comics rarely was more than mediocre.

Superman has a bit of fun with a firing squad in one of his earliest (1939) comic strip adventures.

Many of the best writers and artists were overseas, fighting the real war.

Newspaper comic strips were always recognized as something read by everyone, but from the beginnings of the new medium, comic books were perceived as a format for children. In order to help children participate more fully in the stories, superheroes were given teenage sidekicks, such as Batman's Robin, Captain America's Bucky, Wonder Woman's Wonder Girl, and the Human Torch's Toro.

Until the end of World War II, superheroes had plenty of fighting to do, and were very popular. Comic books and their heroes promoted the war effort by battling the enemy and encouraging readers to purchase war bonds. After the war, however, the superheroes seemed as confused as their creators about what to do next. There was no longer a genuine enemy to fight and, as a bunch, the costumed brawlers battled aimlessly.

In postwar America, society was changing as well. A new American subgroup, the "Teen-ager," was defined by the media and marketers when this term was coined in 1945. Segments of the entertainment industry, such as popular music, began to be produced for consumption by this newly defined group, those in the period between childhood and adulthood. They were the first generation to have grown up with comic books, and they liked them. As a result, comic books appeared everywhere teens hung out.

Despite the talent pool within the comic book industry, few professionals saw the field as a real career. Comic books were the lowest rung of the cultural ladder; the pay was poor, the production shoddy. Given the opportunity, many moved on. One prominent comic book writer and artist who broke out of the comic book industry was Jack Cole. Cole's major contribution to the comic book field was the creation of Plastic Man, a superhero who could stretch and mold his body into any shape. The stories were full of

Jack Cole certainly knew how to have fun while drawing his comics, especially his most famous creation, *Plastic Man*.

irreverence and quirky humor, and Cole's highly individualistic work demonstrated that an artist's personality could be expressed through the comic book medium. Cole moved on to become one of *Playboy* magazine's first cartoonists. Some comic book artists followed him into the world of magazine illustration if they were good enough. Others, such as Jack Kirby, continued working in the comic book field, exploring different genres, because they liked the comic book method of storytelling.

As the 1940s drew to a close, interest in superheroes waned. But if they could find subjects that appealed to them, comic book publishers had a new group of readers who were in the process of remaking popular entertainment and who could secure the future sales of the medium: teenagers.

You've got trouble, right here in River City.
—Harold Hill, *The Music Man*

The 1950s
The Shadow of McCarthyism

In the 1950s, a new era dawned for the comic book industry as comics publishers began to focus on new genres of titles and a new audience. As America put World War II further and further behind it, interest in superheroes decreased. Superheroes had enthusiastically battled the Axis powers, but the public's attitude toward Korean War was far more ambivalent. For the most part, the superheroes stayed out of the conflict. Instead, the comic book response to the war in Korea might best be represented by Harvey Kurtzman's *Two-Fisted Tales,* a meticulously researched war comic book that unflinchingly depicted the horrors of war rather than glorifying it.

The comic book industry invested in other genres: funny animal stories, romance comics, and crime and horror titles. The inventive and adaptable Jack Kirby, together with his partner Joe Simon, brought the romance genre to comics in the late 1940s, helping to broaden the medium's potential appeal. Funny animal comics entertained the kids that returning G.I.s were producing in abundance, while romance, crime, and horror comic books were published with a teen audience in mind. The romance story was hugely popular and, in the context of the 1950s, reinforced conservative social values. Horror and crime comics, on the other hand, dealt with topics that by their nature are transgressive, disturbing, and can lead readers to ask questions about social norms and the limits of authority.

Although the major companies which had ridden to the top of the industry on the success of superheroes like Superman, Batman and Captain America continued to dominate the comic book business, a new player emerged: EC Comics. EC Comics had originally been named Educational Comics, and had published such titles as *Picture Stories from the Bible,* comic book adaptations that were meant to be uplifting, but tended more toward the stultifying. The company was owned by Max Gaines, who had been instrumental in publishing the first comic book, *Famous Funnies,* in 1933. When Gaines died in 1947, his son William inherited the company. The new Gaines changed the direction of the company and the course of the comic book industry by focusing on horror comics. Where Gaines the father had published *Pictures Stories from American History* and *Animal Fables,* his son published *Tales from the Crypt* and *The Haunt of Fear.* EC no longer stood for Educational Comics, but rather Entertaining Comics. The EC books were better drawn and better written than their contemporaries, perhaps because William Gaines was a young man and questioned authority himself, and because he paid more than other companies. As a result, EC attracted some of the most innovative talent in the comics field.

The kids loved EC's books. Teenagers are always fascinated with death and violence, and EC's books were bloodier than their counterparts. And the books offered something that just wasn't available anywhere else—a subversive attitude. The underlying message of EC comic book stories was clear for those with the eyes to read it: the façade America was living in the 1950s was a sham. In the world of EC Comics, parents divorced, politicians

EC's lineup ranged from the bloody, ultra-violent-in-its-day western *Betsy,* by master artist Jack Davis ...

were corrupt, and children were far from innocent. Of course, in an EC Comic book, divorce was not the only cause of marital break-ups—murdering your spouse did the trick as well. The tensions of the nuclear age formed the subtext for war stories in comic books like *Shock Suspenstories* that showed the reader that the next world war would have no winner, and that the whole human race would be the loser. EC's lineup expanded to include such science fiction titles as *Weird Science Fantasy* and a variety of crime comic books. The same dark beauty in the artwork and subversive social subtexts in the stories were found in titles in these genres as well.

EC's most lasting contribution to the comics field was *MAD* magazine. Produced under the direction of Harvey Kurtzman, a veteran humorist who had worked for several comic book publishers, *MAD* initially satirized the comic book industry. Prior to *MAD,* there had been no consistent satire appearing in comic books. Many of the same readers who liked EC's horror books delighted in *MAD*. The James Dean film *Rebel Without a Cause* expressed many of the same social ambiguities of the 1950s, but for many teenagers, an early rallying point was EC Comics. Teens were not the only readers of comic books during the 1950s. During World War II, the United States military had supplied the armed forces with comic books as entertainment and evidence of homefront support, and by the end of the war many soldiers were hooked on words-and-pictures storytelling.

This is not to suggest that other comic book publishing houses had little impact on mass culture in the 1950s, but they had a background role. Romance stories depicting domestic tranquility balanced out the subverting influence of EC comics, and a few superheroes either expanded their own mythology or battled the Cold War, but much of the energy the comics industry created in the 1950s could be traced back to EC (or its imitators) who produced moody, weird fantasy stories for which readers pried coins out of their pockets.

…to Al Feldstein's and Wally Wood's sex-horror, *Came the Dawn*. Both stories pushed their share of buttons and boundaries.

In 1954, psychiatrist Fredric Wertham published a book about troubled American youth, *Seduction of the Innocent.* He cited more than one cause for youthful rebellion, but he pinpointed the influence of comic books as a motivating factor in youthful disturbance. A practicing psychiatrist, Wertham noted that comic books were found in the rooms of teen suicides. He also argued that a steady diet of comic books would ruin an adolescent's taste for fine literature. Comic books, he believed, were too violent, too sexual, too bloody, and openly showed disrespect for authority. Comic books incited rather than reflected youthful aggression. *Seduction of the Innocent* was the culmination of several years of work on the part of Wertham, who had become a recognized speaker on the topic by the time his book reached publication.

Wertham's book caused quite a stir, and dovetailed nicely with the anticommunist sentiment that hypnotized the country. Although Wertham never explicitly linked comic books with communism, the same political currents that led to Hollywood's blacklist now flowed against the smaller and more vulnerable comic book industry. The United States Senate held hearings on comic books and youth. In fear of being shut down, comic book publishers banded together and formed a trade organization to deal with the crisis. The new group, called the Comic Magazine Association of America, then created a series of regulations governing acceptable comic book material, set up an agency to oversee the program, and prayed. Under the new guidelines, called the Comics Code, women were to be properly clad, authority figures respected, and the violence toned down. EC Comics, whose product line had been a catalyst for Wertham's charges, was soon out of the comic book business. Seeing the handwriting on the wall, publisher Gaines responded by upgrading his premier satire comic book, *MAD,* to a magazine format, thus avoiding the regulations of the CMAA and achieving greater financial success and social impact than he ever would have in the comics business.

There was at least one advantage to the new regulations. The boom in sales in crime and horror comics in the 1950s had led to the publication of a lot of sensationalistic material that was produced hurriedly and with little care. The quality level of comic book product rose once the sensationalistic stories that flooded much of the comic book market had been minimized. Comic book publishers tried their hand at different genres whose stories could entertain within the confines of the regulations imposed by the Comics Code. But the underlying messages—that the authority figures were always right, that no police officer was corrupt, that parents lived in marital bliss—were false ones, and the kids knew it. The escapist trip that comic books had always provided survived both Dr. Wertham's charges and McCarthyism, but the energy was gone. Comic books had lost their social relevance.

Fiction is like a spider's web, attached ever so slightly
perhaps, but still attached to life at all four corners.
—Virginia Woolf

The 1960s
Troubled Heroes for Troubled Times

Surprisingly, the 1960s became a vibrant period for American comic books. To recover from the aftermath of the 1950s, the comic book industry had to reinvent itself. Restrictions imposed by the Comics Code made it impossible to tell many of the kinds of stories that had been most successful in the 1950s. Teens and older readers had been attracted to the crime and horror stories in published by EC and other companies, but now these were gone. However, and much to the surprise of those who worked in the industry, one type of story that did work well in the sanitized environment was the superhero story. DC Comics had revived *The Flash* ("The fastest man alive") in 1956, and the book sold. More superheroes followed, some recreations of earlier heroes and some completely new. DC had an army of good guys perennially fighting an army of bad guys. Of course, no one could ever really win, because then the fun would be over.

EC had left the comic book business to concentrate on *MAD* magazine, and other companies had closed. DC's success with superhero stories did not go unnoticed. Marvel Comics, which had published superheroes under a variety of corporate names in the past, was one of DC Comics's remaining competitors,. Stan Lee, Marvel's editor and head writer, decided to create a competing band of superheroes. Lee had been a comics writer for over twenty years, and wanted to write something more complex than simplistic children's stories. He decided that the new Marvel heroes would be as closely grounded in the real world as it was possible for costumed superheroes to be. This meant that these heroes would experience the problems everyday people face as well as the problems that went with battling super-villains. Because the 1960s was a period of anxiety stemming from fears of nuclear war, most of Marvel's heroes were empowered as a result of nuclear accidents, offering an upside to the arms race.

WHAT DO I DO **NOW**? I'VE NEVER BEEN BEATEN BEFORE! BUT **THIS** TIME, MY SPIDER POWERS WERE NOT ENOUGH! IS THIS THE END OF **SPIDER-MAN**?

Who did Spider-Man beat up more … the criminals, or himself?

Marvel's most successful character was teen science wiz Peter Parker, also known as the Spectacular Spider-Man, who became a superhero out of a sense of guilt.

Parker supported his aging Aunt May and was as concerned about paying his electric bill as defeating the bad guy. In addition to being an innovator, Lee was a genuinely funny writer who imbued his stories with tragedy as well as humor. Most of his heroes cracked sarcastic jokes while taking punches on the chin, and watched the girl go off with the other guy as the story closed. This combination appealed to older teens. Other prominent Marvel heroes were the Fantastic Four, Thor, and the Uncanny X-Men. One of the members of the Fantastic Four team was the Thing, a man forever trapped in a freakish body. This character was the first tragic superhero in comics.

Lee didn't build the Marvel universe alone. Two artists were critical in bringing Lee's superhero vision to life: Jack Kirby and Steve Ditko. Kirby was the main artist and mastermind behind most of the new heroes. Like Lee, Kirby was a comic book veteran who'd paid his dues. In addition to trying his hand at almost every genre of comics over the years, Kirby had cocreated Captain America, the super-patriot, in 1941. Perhaps better than anyone else working in comics at the time, Kirby understood that the appeal of superheroes was power. As a result, the Marvel books were more violent, but also more realistic within the boundaries of the superhero fantasy world, than their competitors. Artist Steve Ditko, who created Spider-Man along with Lee, was a master at figure drawing, and drew moody illustrations with vibrant designs that recalled the canvases of the Pop artists. Marvel was hip. As Marvel's popularity grew, Lee became a lecturer on college campuses, a sign that superhero comics were pushing their way off the drugstore spin racks.

Another significant development within the comic book industry during the 1960s was the creation of comics fandom. With the success of superheroes, publishers understood that there was a large readership of adults who recalled superheroes fondly from their childhoods. Beginning in the 1960s, comic book fans gathered in hotels discussing and buying comic books as well as shaking hands with professional comic book creators. One result of meeting other fans in this way was the creation of fanzines, magazines about comic books. Comic book conventions and fanzines assured comic book readers that Dr. Wertham had been wrong; they weren't delinquents or crazy, in fact, several of them had gone on to achieve success in real life, but they still liked comic books.

One of the rallying points of comic fandom was Jules Feiffer's book, *The Great Comic Book Heroes,* which was published in 1965. The book included a lengthy memoir of Feiffer's childhood love of superheroes, some social commentary, and a selection of vintage superhero stories from the comic books of Feiffer's youth. Published during the nostalgia craze, the book had a surprisingly strong impact. It was reviewed on the front page of *The New York Herald Tribune's* book review section and sold well. Perhaps most startling was Feiffer's assertion that comic books, as part of junk culture, served a purpose. In a way, they were good for you.

Jules Feiffer, a cartoonist, playwright, and novelist whose work had appeared in numerous publications, notably *Playboy* and the *Village Voice,* had been offered *The Great Comic Book Heroes* by aspiring novelist E. L. Doctorow, then editor at Dial. The contract negotiation, according to Feiffer, "took about ten minutes." The project was easily accomplished because "DC opened its archives." One unexpected result of the book was the resurrection of the comics career of cartoonist Will Eisner. Feiffer had started his own career in Eisner's shop, and he squeezed a *Spirit* story into the nostalgic volume otherwise filled with tales of Batman, Wonder Woman, and Superman. This single *Spirit* story was a revelation to readers who had been unfamiliar with Eisner's work. In the context of this volume, it was clear that his

Feiffer's *The Great Comic Book Heroes.*

Spirit was a more complex creation than other comic book heroes. The interest generated by Feiffer's book led to reprinting of the *Spirit* stories, and ultimately to Eisner's return to comics.

Zap Comix. 'Nuff said.

The last major force in comic book culture during the 1960s was the underground comix movement. The undergrounds were comic books written and drawn by young adults for their peers. They questioned social mores, encouraged opposition to the Vietnam War, told the story of the sexual revolution, and presented autobiographical tales. There had never been anything like this in comic books before, and the impact of the American undergrounds was felt in comic books throughout the world. Of course, these comic books could not be sold on newsstands or in drugstore spin racks. They were totally and intentionally opposed in every way to the standards set by the Comics Code. The first few undergrounds were sold on street corners, but they quickly found an outlet in the head shops that sprang up across the country to sell hippie paraphernalia.

The underground comix movement had its first great success in 1968, when artist Robert Crumb created *Zap Comics.* The book was so influential that for a time "zap comics" was a term used interchangeably with underground comix. The roots of the underground were the EC comics of the 1950s, particularly Harvey Kurtzman's early issues of *MAD,* but there was also a powerful influence from EC's horror and science fiction titles in many of the new comics.

The undergrounds were unexpectedly successful. During the late 1960s, it wasn't unusual for an underground comic to sell 30,000 to 50,000 copies. Probably the best-selling underground series was Gilbert Shelton's *The Fabulous Furry Freak Brothers,* which was rumored to have sold over 100,000 copies.

As the 1960s drew to a close, the comics industry had adapted handily to the confines of the Comics Code. Mainstream publishers had found ways to more creatively tell stories while adhering to the Code, a comic book fan culture was growing, and the hippie revolution had found a way to put its stamp on the comics medium. The best was yet to come.

Will you take me as I am?
—Joni Mitchell

The Comic Book Store
Fans Find a Home

In the early 1970s, a network of comic book specialty stores began to grow throughout the United States. This new system of selling comic books, where specialized stores sold back issues and also offered an alternative to newsstands for the sale of new comics, eventually came to be called the direct market. The specialty shop was an outgrowth of the comic book conventions held during the 1960s and early 1970s, which had demonstrated the growing breadth and diversity of the comic book market. Comic book publishing houses sold comic books to these specialty stores on a nonreturnable basis. Comics sold on newsstands can be returned to the publisher for credit if they don't sell. In the direct market, comic store owners receive a larger discount but could not return any unsold books.

In order for a store to succeed, the owner had to have a clear sense of his customer base. This new method was good news for comic book publishers because it gave them a bottom-line number of magazines that they knew had been sold and would not be returned. Over time, the comic book specialty shop practically replaced spin rack

Evan Dorkin's *Eltingville Comic-Book, Science-Fiction, Fantasy, Horror, and Role Playing Club* leaves even the biggest fans…

comic book distribution. The concept of the comic book store was in part inspired by the head shops of the 1960s, where underground comix had found a profitable niche alongside the black light posters and rolling papers. The brisk sales of comic books at fan conventions also demonstrated the strength of the comics market. Entrepreneurs saw that by going directly to the readers, a profit could be made. However, most of the early comic book shop owners were not underground comix readers, but science fiction fans and dedicated readers of mainstream comics, particularly the EC line the 1950s. In the early days of the development of the comic shop system, there was little room in the stores for underground comix.

To a comic book fan, the comic book store was a kind of heaven: a room full of comic books, populated by other people who liked them without any judgments.

The comic book specialty shop influenced the direction of comic book publishing dramatically. Because magazine print runs were at least in part determined by the orders retailers placed, publishers had a much clearer sense of who was reading their books. And as their readership changed, publishers were able redirect their storylines accordingly. The comic book store venue demonstrated convincingly that grown-ups still read comics. As result, publishers experimented with superhero concepts aimed at older readers. The success of the underground comix movement and Marvel's popularity on college campuses proved that comics weren't just being read by twelve-year-old boys. Through the new venue of the comic book store, publishers gleaned a sense of who these readers were. New companies sprang up. Some, such as NBM, had no interest in superhero stories or undergrounds, but had been influenced by European comic culture. Others, such as First, tried their hand at superhero and adventure stories, competing with big companies such as Marvel and DC for readers.

The comic book specialty shop was good news for comics publishing. It opened up a market for a more diverse range of comics, and new companies like Fantagraphics and Warp

…wondering just how much of the obscure trivia …

Graphics rose to meet the challenge. Some underground publishers, like Kitchen Sink Press, adapted to the new market by diversifying their lines in order to attract comic book readers uninterested in the undergrounds. At its height, during the 1980s, there were as many as 5,000 comic book specialty shops throughout the United States.

…cited in the Eisner award-winning story *Bring Me the Head of Boba Fett* came right off the top of Dorkin's head.

Underground comix did not transition well into the comic book specialty shop. Most store managers weren't fans of the undergrounds and concentrated on mainstream comics. Other factors, such as a 1973 Supreme Court decision which gave local communities the power to define obscenity, left both comic book shop and head shop owners terrified. They already operated at the fringes of society, and now they no longer had federal protection. By the late 1970s, the undergrounds had virtually disappeared because of the lack of a workable distribution system. But the movement had left its mark. Some comics produced for the mainstream, such as Frank Miller's *Batman: The Dark Knight Returns* were growing more political in their statements, while other decidedly underground comix, such as Art Spiegelman's *Raw,* continued to be published and even attracted attention beyond the confines of the comics field. By the mid 1980s, the comic book specialty shop had become the primary vehicle by which comics made their way to the reading public.

I must trust what was given to me if I am
to trust anything.
—W.S. Merwin

The Graphic Novel
Comics Take Themselves Seriously

The first modern "graphic novel" was written and illustrated by veteran cartoonist Will Eisner, who coined the term while trying to persuade the editors at Bantam Books to publish the book-length comic book. Bantam declined, but the term stuck. Will Eisner's graphic novel, *A Contract with God and Other Tenement Stories,* was no traditional novel in more ways than one. Not only did the illustrations convey most of the narrative elements within the story, but the book consisted of four thematically linked short stories that together formed a portrait of working-class Jewish life in New York during the Great Depression.

Eisner had a long history in and out of the comics industry. He began his career in 1936, when his studio, Eisner & Iger, supplied original stories to early comic book publishers. In 1940 he sold his business and began producing a small comic book supplement designed to be syndicated to Sunday newspapers. The supplement featured the Spirit, a masked crime fighter whom the world thought dead. The stories were by turns tragic, ironic, and humorous, and appealed to adult readers as well as children. After *The*

Is *this* how God does business? Frimme Hersh tackles the slippery issue of faith in the title story from *Contract With God.*

Spirit ceased publication in 1952, Eisner built a company that supplied businesses and the military with educational material using the comic book format. But Eisner's comic book work, particularly *The Spirit,* remained legendary among comic book fans. When Jules Feiffer included a section on Will Eisner as well as a Spirit story in *The Great Comic Book Heroes,* Eisner's creation was viewed with renewed interest. Feiffer's book was followed by a feature article on Eisner and *The Spirit* in the *New York Herald Tribune* in 1966, creating an even greater curiosity about what had happened to this pioneering and innovative comic book artist.

One comics fan turned comics convention organizer decided to find out. Phil Seuling, who spearheaded the comic book specialty shop movement, invited Will Eisner to be a guest at a comic book convention in New York City in 1971. At the conference, Eisner met Art Spiegelman, and cartoonist and publisher Denis Kitchen. The environment inspired Eisner: here were young cartoonists using the comics medium in the ways that he'd always hoped it could be used, as a vehicle for personal and political statements rather than as a medium restricted to regurgitated genre stories. Eisner characterized the underground comix movement as being equivalent to "the French underground" during World War II, liberating comics from the bonds that had kept it from achieving its full potential as an art.

In 1972, shortly after attending the comic book convention, Eisner sold his interest in his educational comics company and rededicated himself to the advancement of the comics medium. Inspired by the innovations of the underground cartoonists, Eisner said he was intent on pushing the form "into areas that had not been done before."

Eisner didn't hesitate to depict real life—even its less-than-appealing qualities—in *Cookalein,* from *Contract with God.*

His reasoning was clear. Eisner observed that children who had read comics in the 1940s would be in their thirties in the mid-1970s. Those people hadn't given up on comics, but the comics field had given up on them. So he responded by writing and drawing *A Contract with God and Other Tenement Stories,* a thematically related collection told in the voices of several characters, a novel in the sense that Sherwood Anderson's *Winesburg, Ohio* is a novel. The first story, "A Contract with God," recounts the life of Frimme Hersh, who has buried his daughter Rachele. Hersh believes that he and God had a contract, and as long as he remained pious, his family was safe. Thinking that God had broken their covenant, Hersh becomes a real estate baron, and then asks a group of rabbis to negotiate a new contract between God and himself. Reluctantly, the rabbis accede to the request, but Hersh dies before he can test the new contract. In the next story, "The Street Singer," an unemployed singer is taken in by an equally down-and-out promoter. Although baffled by her professional and amorous interest in him, the singer decides to work with the promoter only to realize that he'd forgotten where she lives. "The Super" tells the story of how a young girl remorselessly outwits the apartment building superintendent through innuendo of sexual harassment, inadvertently causing his suicide. The final story, "Cookalein," focuses on the fifteenth summer of Willie, who is sent off to a summer resort, where he traumatically loses his virginity to an older, married woman. When Willie returns to his family at the end of the summer he is a wiser, more knowing person. Throughout these stories, no judgments are rendered. Eisner is more interested in depicting characters and their situations in life than in leading the readers to any kind of moral judgments.

Not only was the subject matter new to comic book readers, the presentation was fresh as well. Rather than crowding the pages with panels detailing character movements, the drawings were large, focusing on facial expression, and the panels opened outward, almost beyond the page.

A Contract with God and Other Tenement Stories was first published by a small house, Baronet Publishing, in 1978. When Baronet failed, Kitchen Sink Press, which had been republishing Eisner's Spirit stories, picked up the book. In the late 1990s, Kitchen Sink Press went out of business and *Contract* again found a new publisher, DC Comics. The book has been continuously in print since 1978. Working on *Contract,* Eisner felt he had "completed something I started out to do a long time ago," and that his innovative new work "was on the right course." In the intervening years since the publication of *Contract,* Eisner has gone on to become one of the field's most prolific graphic novelists, but with the publication of *Contract,* he had charted a new course for comics and ensured that the name he had chosen for this form would become universally accepted.

For those who like this sort of thing, this is the sort
of thing they like.
—Max Beerbohm

Trade Publishers and Comics
An Uneasy Alliance

A Contract with God was the first original comic work of art published by an American trade book publisher. However, books presented in comic book format had been a side interest of the trade publishing houses for some time. In the late 1930s, Jean De Brunhoff's noted series of children's books about Babar sometimes appeared in comic book format. Dressed up collections of "classic" comic strips such as Herriman's *Krazy Kat* (with an introduction by poet e. e. cummings) became available in the 1960s. Throughout the 1960s and 1970s, books collecting Charles Schulz's newspaper strip *Peanuts* were perennially popular. A minister, Robert Short, rode the wave of the strip's popularity with a highly successful book of his own, a short religious treatise entitled *The Gospel According to Peanuts*. Other comic strip collections such as *Beetle Bailey* were published in the wake of the success of *Peanuts*. Maurice Sendak's picture book, *In the Night Kitchen,* an ode to Mickey Mouse, was awarded the Caldecott Honor in 1971. Europe's most successful series of comics in book form was brought to America by the publisher Little, Brown, which introduced Herge's superb adventure series *Tintin* in 1973.

By turns humorous and dramatic, the stories of boy reporter Tintin and his dog Snowy captivated American readers. Perhaps the best known cartoonist publishing with the trade houses was Raymond Briggs, whose 1978 book *The Snowman,* a wordless drama about a boy and his snowman, won several honors. Briggs followed the success of *The Snowman* with a chilling cautionary tale of a nuclear war, *When the Wind Blows,* in 1981.

The general public appeared to trust books presented in comic book format when these books were sponsored by a major publisher. These books were considered safe and educational. If young people read these, it was thought, it could encourage them to move on to reading books composed primarily of text.

That perception altered slightly with the publication of Jules Feiffer's comic book novel *Tantrum* in 1979. The story was sobering. Leo, middle aged and heavy with responsibility, wills himself back to babyhood while retaining adult sensibilities and desires. After his transformation, baby Leo finds no comfort in his wife and children and looks for consolation from his sister-in-law, Joyce. But Leo finds that Joyce's response to middle age is as terrifying as his own; Joyce is starving herself in order to look young.

Men of all ages are so often accused of acting like little boys.

After Leo feeds Joyce back to health, he reverts back to middle age as a result of adult sexual attraction. Returning to his family, Leo learns that his wife, too, has learned to revert to infancy. Leo becomes a baby again and the two escape their children and their burdened lives.

Feiffer's cartooning was not new to the reading public. In addition to being Will Eisner's assistant, his cartoons had appeared in *Playboy* and *The Village Voice*. Feiffer's work made its impact through uncluttered drawings combined with ironic punch lines. He'd also been a playwright, a novelist, a screenwriter, and an illustrator for *The Phantom Tollbooth,* a classic children's novel.

But *Tantrum* was a striking departure for the cartoonist. Not only were the themes expressed in *Tantrum* startling, the drawings were bold. The illustrations possessed a kind of electricity which allowed them to open into each other almost breathlessly. The combination of the tortured theme and the magnetic drawings made for compelling reading.

Although one might think that the changes occurring within the comic book industry had influenced Feiffer, he was for the most part, unaware of them. *Tantrum* grew out of

With *Tantrum,* Feiffer not only capitalized on this concept, he justified it!

23

Feiffer's turning fifty, and his unrealized desire to do something more with the comic book format.

Tantrum also changed the way Feiffer drew. Prior to doing *Tantrum*, Feiffer had penciled out his drawings then inked over them. To convey the necessary sense of urgency, the cartoonist eliminated the pencil step and drew directly in ink. *Tantrum* was a breakthrough book for readers, and it proved to be a personal artistic breakthrough for Feiffer as well. What made *Tantrum* work so well, Feiffer believed, was that "it was a combination of all the skills I'd learned from all the fields I'd worked in." After creating *Tantrum,* Feiffer felt that he had changed as an artist, and subsequently his drawings "took more risks."

Vision is the art of seeing things invisible.
—Jonathan Swift

Opening the Gates
The Comics Field Grows

The comic book store changed the way readers thought about comic books, and it also changed the ways that comic book publishing houses perceived themselves. Despite the fact that the comic book store was considered suspect by mainstream culture, it offered cartoonists an informed audience for their work, something they'd never had before. New comic book publishers sprang up, most offering imitations of successful books published by bigger companies. There was an electric energy, perhaps because it was possible to break into comics. *The Comics Journal,* a magazine dedicated to serious study of comics as an art form, was founded by Fantagraphics Books in 1976. The distributors who bought books from publishers and then resold them to comic book stores had gotten into the business because they were fans of the medium. They were approachable if you had a product that seemed appealing. Suddenly, it seemed, anyone who could draw could break into comics publishing.

This environment allowed very small, gremlin, companies to flourish. Revenues from the network of comic book stores could support a couple or a small staff. Warp Graphics,

Questioning the unquestionability of elfin love in Elfquest.

started by Richard and Wendy Pini, was one such company. Begun in 1976, Warp Graphics published an androgynous fantasy series, *Elfquest,* about a race of elves searching for their homeland. Wendy Pini was a successful professional science fiction and fantasy illustrator, but she wanted to publish her own original comics work. The idea for *Elfquest* had been brewing in her mind since childhood, and she served as both writer and artist for the series. Richard played the role of publisher and editor.

Elfquest had a look and feel that set it apart from all of its contemporaries in the comics field. The characters in *Elfquest* were sleek and strong, possessing both male and female attributes. In her work, Wendy combined the masculine strength of the American superhero—Jack Kirby was her artistic mentor—with American and European fantasy and children's book illustration. Drawing on elements of Native American traditions, European fairy tales, and pieces of different cultural backgrounds, *Elfquest* was wholly American, and had a large female readership. In the early 1980s, the *Elfquest* comic book was selling in the neighborhood of 100,000 copies per issue. In 1981 the *Elfquest* collections in trade paperback format, now published in full color, landed in bookstores. It was the first graphic novel series to push its way out of the comic book marketplace. Promoted primarily by word of mouth, the book made its way into public libraries in 1984. *Elfquest* continued to expand, branching out into prose novels and a series of collectible figures. *Elfquest* connected so strongly with such a varied group of readers, the Pinis believe, because "it was a reflection of what we were going through in symbolic fantasy clothing." Amazingly, because the comic book industry was in a period of redefinition and transition, tiny companies such as Warp Graphics had a major impact on the comics field.

Two companies brought a European influence over to these shores, NBM and Catalan. Small, but bigger than Warp Graphics, NBM had been started because one of the owners, Terry Nantier, had lived in Europe and was influenced and impressed by the plethora of greatly successful graphic albums published there. These albums were longer than American comic books, totaling 48-64 pages. Also unlike their American counterparts, they were beautifully produced, with excellent color reproduction, good quality paper, and were

NBM's very own *The Call of the Stars*.

generally published as hardcover books. Graphic albums were primarily collections of sophisticated stories appealing directly to adults, while ignoring the superhero genre entirely. Nantier reasoned that adults living in the United States would find these books interesting as well, and his assumption was correct. NBM became America's first graphic novel publisher, initiating its Flying Buttress imprint in 1976 by making, amongst others, Enki Bilal's *The Call of the Stars* available to literary comics readers. NBM's and Catalan's books made an impression on sophisticated comic book readers, and they served as an introduction to European style comic book storytelling for the next generation of American cartoonists as they developed their own storytelling idioms. Following the European example, NBM continually sought avenues for book sales outside of the comic book store venue. Because they were one of the pioneers of the graphic novel form, and because many of their graphic novels looked and felt like trade books, they experienced some success placing their books in bookstores and public libraries.

The experiments continued. Eclipse, another small publishing house trying to make its mark alongside DC and Marvel Comics, released one of the first graphic novels, *Sabre* by Don McGregor and Paul Gulacy, in 1979. *Sabre* told a mature adventure story, and the creative team was hot, so book sales were impressive. As a form, the graphic novel was beginning to catch on.

Cerebus, a creation of Dave Sim and Gerhard at Aardvark-Vanaheim, was another fantasy series, although much different from *Elfquest*. The protagonist was an aardvark, and the initial intention of the comic book was to parody the sword and sorcery craze raging throughout mainstream comics throughout the 1970s. In 1980, Sim collected a group of issues of *Cerebus* into an extensive trade paperback which he called a phone book, and sold it directly to comic book stores without involving a middleman. Many were surprised when these phone books sold, but the concept was becoming clear: readers were interested in bound comic book collections, whether they were called phone books, comic book novels,

Cerebus the aardvark: aalways aangry!

The Teenage Mutant Ninja Turles cash cow.

albums, or graphic novels.

Another series founded by a small company, Mirage Studios, the *Teenage Mutant Ninja Turtles,* proved successful. The brainchild of creative partners Kevin Eastman and Peter Laird, who wrote and drew the book together, the *Turtles* began as a parody of the ninja craze sweeping the country in the early and mid-1980s. Laird and Eastman partnered with a sophisticated media and licensing representative, and soon the *Turtles* seemed omnipresent: as toys, lunchbox decorations, an animated TV show, and a box office attraction.

Where companies such as Warp Graphics were riding the changing wave of comics, Mirage Studios seemed to rise out of the comics field effortlessly. Although denied the critical acclaim offered *Elfquest,* Eastman and Laird enjoyed the kind of financial success most comic book creators only dream about, and the original comic book series was collected into a set of easy-to-buy graphic novels. The key to the success of the *Teenage Mutant Ninja Turtles* lay in the visual humor. Laird and Eastman had been inspired by comic book creators Frank Miller and Jack Kirby, but unlike many followers of these artists, they were influenced by both the action and the humor of their work. The books had a fun sense of exaggerated violence, and it proved possible to transform them into a hugely successful animated series. In that format, each turtle was remarkably similar to the others, but different enough to satisfy a child. The Turtles were soon an international phenomenon.

Finally, a small company trying for a piece of the comic book pie was Dark Horse Comics. Mike Richardson, the company's founder, had owned a chain of successful comic book stores and branched out into publishing in 1986. From the start, Dark Horse attracted some of the comic industry's top talent, and their books were well supported within the comic book marketplace. Their way out of the comic book field didn't come until the 1990s, when Dark Horse published a series of well-produced graphic novel adaptations of George Lucas's *Star Wars* movies.

The success of these companies demonstrated conclusively that the core of the comic book readership had changed, and their popularity helped convince the major companies, DC and Marvel Comics, to revise their product lines in order to bring lost readers back.

It's up to each generation to write the Iliad anew.
—Alan Garner

The New Heroes
Would You Let This Man Marry Your Sister?

One of the tangible benefits of the comic book store venue for publishers was an increased understanding of who the reading public was. This allowed small presses such as Warp Graphics to thrive, and it made room for major companies to rework their heroes to better fit the mood of the current store clientele. Because superheroes were still popular in the late 1970s, and because the comic book readership was growing into its twenties, the editors at Marvel began to wonder whether or not the superhero genre could be modified to interest adults.

The evidence was there if you looked at it in the right way. The 1978 movie *Superman* was a megahit, and teens and twenty-somethings were the target audience. So Marvel commissioned Frank Miller, an artist fairly new the profession, to write *Daredevil* as well as draw it. Daredevil, "the man without fear," was a weaker version of Marvel's own Spider-Man. Daredevil was blind but his other four senses had been sharpened due to exposure to radiation. In real life he was a lawyer who sometimes defended the very criminals he chased when putting on his red suit. With Frank Miller at the helm, the book took on an entirely different tone as well as a new storyline.

Miller's *Daredevil* was no longer an acrobatic superhero whose stunts were derived from Spider-Man's moves, but instead became a warrior trained in the martial arts. His senses, which had been heightened by radiation, could now detect aspects of the human condition: he could hear a pulse beat jump, and knew if the witness or criminal was telling the truth. But Miller's inventiveness didn't stop there; he created the character Elektra, a ninja assassin whom Daredevil came to love. Electra's employer, The Kingpin, was a criminal mastermind masquerading as a shrewd businessman. Although Miller was doing a superhero book, his real interest was crime fiction, and the *Daredevil* stories became sophisticated crime stories. The necessary heroics were evident, but the stories resembled Will Eisner's *The Spirit* more than a superhero slugfest. Miller's Daredevil didn't outright win; he survived, and for some unfathomable reason, wanted to fight another day.

Miller's artwork offered a break from the overdrawn stories of the late 1970s and early 1980s. Although displaying an extraordinary amount of violence, it was lean and the movements seemed to be choreographed. Frank Miller's *Daredevil* became a major success; it won industry awards and attracted legions of readers, making Miller one of the hottest talents in the comics field.

One of the things the new *Daredevil* book signified was that the content restrictions imposed by the Comics Code were loosening. Both Marvel and DC had tested the restrictions before: in the early 1970s one *Spider-Man* story focused on drug use. Mention of drug use was forbidden by the Comics Code, and the issue went to print without their stamp of approval. Not to be outdone, DC Comics presented the readers with an affecting story about Speedy, the Green Arrow's boy partner, who had become a heroin addict. The restrictions had become less rigid. In fact, the seal of approval by the Comics Code became much more arbitrary; many comic books in the 1980s regularly appeared without the Code's seal.

At roughly the same time as Marvel was toying with the Daredevil superhero concept, DC Comics was conducting an experiment of its own. British writer Alan Moore had been hired to rework *Swamp Thing,* a series about a scientist whose experiments gone awry had turned him into a swamp creature. *Swamp Thing* was one of the comic book industry's endless versions of the mythic bogeyman creature. Artist Steve Bissette worked with Moore, and their version of the Swamp Thing displayed a greater depth of human emotion. At the same time, the Swamp Thing became more powerful, a kind of superhero whose powers were derived from its nature as a creature of the swamp. Under the team of Moore and Bissette, Swamp Thing became almost a nature god, and the stories naturally explored environmental concerns, while the character personified the outsider.

Swamp Thing became a hit for DC. Moore's scripts revealed a human being inside the swamp creature, and Bissette's art was deliciously murky and seemed almost to flow off the page. Just as Miller's *Daredevil* reminded readers of a detective story while telling a superhero tale, *Swamp Thing* reminded readers of a horror book even though it departed radically from the horror tradition. The success of both *Daredevil* and *Swamp Thing* changed the direction of mainstream comics: publishers understood that readers wanted more complicated, more realistic and more involved stories. Another change was that, although Moore wrote but did not draw *Swamp Thing*, he was considered to be the strongest creative force behind the stories. This was the first time the writer of a comic book had received more notice and acclaim for a successful comic book than the artist. Although Miller both wrote and drew *Daredevil*, he became known as a writer. This shift from focusing on the artist to promoting the

Steve Bissette's version of DC's Swamp Thing.

comic book writer encouraged writers, specifically Miller and Moore, to take more risks.

There were other noteworthy experiments going on as well. Marvel had given one of their top-of-the-line creators, Jim Starlin, the odious task of killing off a weak superhero, Captain Marvel. This was not the famous Fawcett character in the red suit, but a humorless, standard-issue superhero with the same name. Starlin turned in a nice piece of work which proved to be appealing to older readers. In *The Life and Death of Captain Marvel*, the hero doesn't go out in a blaze of glory, but rather falls victim to a cosmic illness in an ending that emphasizes humanity over heroics.

At First Comics, a competitor of Marvel and DC for the attention of older readers, Howard Chaykin was writing and drawing *American Flagg!* Set in the future, the hero Reubin Flagg is both a media star and a ranger. The stories were filled with humor, violence, cinematic visuals, and graphic sex. *American Flagg!* succeeded in capturing the attention of the comics buying audience, and was another book to appear without the approval of the Comics Code.

Although both *Swamp Thing* and *Daredevil* were accomplished works, they turned out to be practice pieces for Moore and Miller, who, within a few years, went on to create comic book stories that paved the way for the acceptance of the graphic novel.

Because of their high visibility within the comics field, both Miller and Moore were allowed a great deal of freedom, and both chose to further experiment with the hero concept. DC Comics lured Miller away from Marvel, and published a solid ninja book of his, *Ronin,* before turning him loose on one of their premier heroes: Batman. Also at DC, Moore turned his attention to creating a world populated with superheroes of his own creation, and teamed with artist Dave Gibbons to bring it to life.

Miller created a novel and deeply cynical Batman story. *Batman: The Dark Knight Returns* was built on a new premise: as much as Batman fought crime for altruistic reasons, he was also psychologically compelled to do so. The story featured Batman at age

Frank Miller's fifty-year-old Batman, from *The Dark Knight Returns*

fifty, ten years into retirement, reemerging to save Gotham City from his nemesis, the Joker. At fifty, Batman isn't the athlete of his youth. Robin has died, and he must recruit a new Robin. Perhaps capturing the feminist sentiment of the times, the new Robin is female. In true comic book tradition, Batman does save Gotham City, but it's a bleak world that he saves. He hasn't won as much as he's survived, and with careful planning he will survive again. The government isn't going to protect you, Miller warns us, you have to do it yourself, and in case you hadn't realized—you don't save people only because it's the right thing to do, you do it because you need the thrill.

The artist as well as the writer, Miller played with the page breakdowns to purposely disorient the reader, and the coloring set the tone for the ultimately dark mood. *Batman: The Dark Knight Returns* was packaged for adult readers, and printed on expensive paper in a "prestige" edition. It appeared first as four individual issues and was collected in one volume in 1987.

Moore offered a somewhat different vision of the superhero mythos in his book *Watchmen.* Teamed with artist Dave Gibbons this time, Moore created a very complex story featuring a group of throwaway characters. In a fantasy world where President Richard Nixon had never been impeached, all superheroes were outlawed. The only exception was Dr. Manhattan, empowered by an atomic experiment, who was allowed to continue only because he worked for the government. The disappearance of Dr. Manhattan demands that the less powerful heroes resume their careers, but they find that the old rules don't work anymore; they are mortal, impotent without a costume, in some cases crazy, and considered somewhat of a joke by the general populace. When, at the climax, Manhattan does return, he is disappointed with humanity. *Watchmen* was seasoned

Nite Owl and Silk Spectre chat about nuclear war and what happened earlier in the evening in issue seven of *Watchmen*

with references to Einstein, the Bible, William Blake, Carl Jung, and Bob Dylan, and a segment of it appeared as a prose memoir of a retired superhero, treats for readers wanting highbrow comic books. Using the superhero genre as a forum, Moore and Gibbons were able to ask questions about the meaning of time and whether or not absolute power corrupts.

As he had done with Steve Bissette while working on *Swamp Thing,* Alan Moore used Gibbons's artistic gifts to further the story. His art is linear and direct, with a literalism that belies the seriousness of the story. Most pages were multipaneled and many contained no words. Artistically, *Watchmen* was more colorful than *Batman: The Dark Knight Returns.* The vision offered in *Watchmen* was, ultimately, more optimistic. *Watchmen* was originally serialized in twelve high-priced issues, and then collected as a graphic novel in 1987. With the duo of *Dark Knight* and *Watchmen,* DC Comics was able to attract readers outside of comic book stores. Articles about the books appeared in *Rolling Stone, Vanity Fair,* the *Los Angeles Times,* and other mainstream publications. In 1988, *Watchmen* was awarded the Hugo, a prestigious science fiction award.

Dark Knight received wider media coverage, sold more, and was ultimately more accessible to mainstream readers than *Watchmen.* The longevity of the Batman character and the popularity of the 1960s TV show made it possible for most readers to jump right into Frank Miller's updated version. To really understand what Moore and Gibbons were saying in *Watchmen,* one had to be familiar with the superhero construct itself. But both *Watchmen* and *Dark Knight* had at least one message in common: don't get caught in a dark alley with someone choosing to wear a mask and fight crime. He wouldn't necessarily turn out to be a nice guy or anyone that you could depend on. In fact, his sanity was probably held together with masking tape.

Sometimes even to live is an act of courage.
—Seneca

Maus
Surviving and Thriving

When Pantheon Books published Art Spiegelman's graphic novel *Maus: A Survivor's Tale* in 1986, the graphic novel landscape was permanently altered. *Maus* featured an extraordinarily complicated narrative that told three stories simultaneously. Spiegelman's parents were survivors of Auschwitz, and it follows them hiding from the Nazis in their native Poland to their capture and their internment in the concentration camp. It also tells the story of the artist's relationship with his eccentric father who, in some ways, was still reliving the war, and the story of Spiegelman himself, who struggled against his family's history.

Told in clear, direct, black and white drawings that depicted Jews as mice, Polish people as pigs, and the Germans as cats, *Maus* deserved serious attention from those outside the insular world of comic book shops. At last there was a book that graphic novel supporters could hold up proudly. *Maus* was a masterpiece. *Maus* existed outside of any normal comic book genre except, if one stretched far enough, funny animal stories. But *Maus* wasn't funny—it was tragic, poignant, and ultimately deeply moving. Jules Feiffer said it was a "remarkable work, awesome in its conception and execution … at one and the same time a novel, a documentary, a memoir, and a comic book." Whatever it was, readers couldn't put it down.

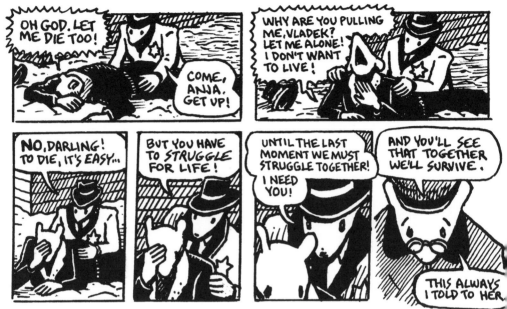

Art Spiegelman's father describes the challenge of living in the Srodula ghetto in *Maus I* …

Maus: A Survivor's Tale had originally been serialized from 1981 through 1986 in the alternative comic book anthology *Raw,* which was coedited by Spiegelman and his wife Francoise Mouly. Earlier incarnations of *Maus* had appeared in the underground press in the 1970s. *Raw* magazine itself had helped prepare the way for the reception of the graphic novel. By recruiting several prominent New York painters to draw stories for various issues, the magazine had boosted the reputation of comics in the world of artists and critics, helping to lead to increased media coverage in the early 1980s.

When Pantheon initially published *Maus,* sales expectations were low. *Maus* wasn't expected to sell any better than their average book. One of the first indicators of the success of *Maus* was Spiegelman's reception at a book signing for an independent book store. Following the book signing, the store manager told Spiegelman that the signing line had stretched out of the store and actually around the city block, and that the signing had been the best attended program that the manager could remember.

Although new to mainstream readers, Art Spiegelman had been a professional cartoonist since the age of sixteen. He was an influential underground cartoonist, important enough that he had had the unusual distinction of an early hardcover collection of his work in the volume *Breakdowns.* Like most underground and alternative cartoonists,

Spiegelman had to supplement the income from his more creative work with a day job. He worked steadily for Topps, a company that produced sports cards and other inserts packed with bubblegum, from 1965 until he resigned over a disagreement related to licensing issues in 1986.

While the public response to *Maus* was clear, the critical reaction was mixed. Although many reviewers praised the book, few understood that the cartoon format was intrinsic to the telling of the story or that, as a cartoonist, Spiegelman paid as much attention to each panel as a novelist such as Philip Roth might pay to the construction of a sentence or paragraph. The fact that *Maus* was loosely linked to Frank Miller's *Batman: The Dark Knight Returns* and Moore and Gibbons's *Watchmen,* sophisticated superhero stories aimed at adults, left some mainstream critics scratching their heads. Both superhero stories were created out of an impulse to contemporize superheroes. Spiegelman created *Maus* to "sort out and put into linear form, the chaos of my own personal history." Spiegelman was clearly influenced by a range of antecedents, both within and outside the comic field. Harvey Kurtzman's work at EC, including the early, formative issues of *MAD* played a role, as did such literary works as George Orwell's political novel *Animal Farm* and the work of Franz Kafka. Less immediately apparent but perhaps equally important were the works of classic cartoonists like George Herriman, the creator of *Krazy Kat,* and

…and the even more difficult obstacles he faced in the concentration camp, Auschwitz, in *Maus II.*

Winsor McKay, the pioneering animator whose best-known comic strip was *Little Nemo*. The darkly powerful work of EC artist Bernie Krigstein also had an impact on Spiegelman's graphic novel.

While *Maus* paid homage to earlier masters, it represented a new breakthrough into the public consciousness. Spiegelman's follow up, *Maus II: From Mauschwitz to the Catskills,* earned him a special Pulitzer Prize in 1992. Along with greater notice came new opportunities, and Spiegelman began working for the *New Yorker* magazine in the mid-1990s. The popularity of both volumes of *Maus* increased throughout the 1990s, and the books became required reading in many school systems. Although useful as an educational tool, *Maus* continued to attract primarily an adult readership. Many new to the graphic novel field found Spiegelman's achievement so deep that they felt no other graphic novel would measure up, and *Maus* became the only graphic novel they had read.

The importance of *Maus* cannot be overstated. The publication and ensuing reception of Spiegelman's book sounded a double alarm within the public discourse. The non-comic book reading public did appreciate sophisticated, rich, visionary storytelling and comic book creators could now raise the bar. If they came up with a compelling enough story which was refined enough in its presentation, cartoonists could break out of the comic book ghetto. But the chance was only there if the cartoonist revealed enough of him- or herself in the telling of the tale, and leapt, as Spiegelman had, fearlessly into the abyss.

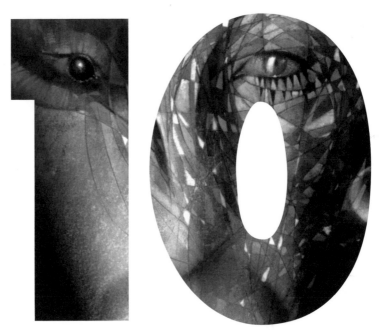

Death was a friend, and sleep was Death's brother.
—John Steinbeck

A New Mythology
The Sandman

In an effort to repeat the successes of *Batman: The Dark Knight Returns* and *Watchmen,* DC Comics began to search for ways to publish sophisticated comics aimed at mature readers. A young british writer, Neil Gaiman, was commissioned to create a dark fantasy series designed to appeal to these readers and to keep them following comics. Gaiman decided to reinvent a 1940s hero, the Sandman, who solved crimes by using sleeping gas. Only Gaiman's Sandman didn't solve crimes. He was the incarnation of dreaming itself, and his power came from the dream world. Gaiman reasoned that if there was a being who embodied dreaming, he would not be alone, but would be joined by other supernaturals who represented the diversity of human conditions. His pantheon ultimately included the seven Endless, all incarnations of very primitive human states. Dream had six siblings: Death, Destruction, Destiny, Desire, Delirium, and Despair. Mythic gods such as Zeus or Isis might come and go but the impulses behind these gods, personified by the Endless, remained. Or, as Gaiman put it, "the joy of genre fiction is undercutting the gods."

Some cartoonists make their mark with a storyline that had percolated in their minds for several years, but *Sandman* had no real origin prior to Gaiman's assignment to write the book. The way *Sandman* evolved was a response to Gaiman's need to keep the storyline flowing on a monthly basis. If the Endless characters were the backbone of the story, then all human traits could be explored. Because the Endless were older than time, all human history could be part of the story as well. History did play a part; historical personages such as William Shakespeare and Marco Polo became characters in the series, as well as mythic figures such as Loki and Lucifer. A cast of contemporary characters balanced out the historical and mythic figures. This mix of familiar historical figures, the supernatural and symbolic but highly personalized Endless, and a diverse cast of contemporary characters lent itself to a series of highly distinctive and engaging stories that delighted readers.

While the Endless considered themselves superior to humanity, they constantly bickered among themselves and ironically exhibited very human traits. Each was a border god; the state each personified was fluid, subject to change. The dream state took one from wakefulness into sleep, Destruction lifted one from peace to violence, and Death took one from this life into the next one. Gaiman adroitly painted the Endless almost as a contemporary family.

Another facet of the series that ultimately contributed to its success was the nature of Gaiman's collaboration with the artists who worked on it. The artistic chores were given to a variety of artists, each with a different style. This constant change pleasantly surprised readers, as Gaiman wrote different storylines accenting the skills the different artists possessed. Some storylines were crowded with shadows because the artist drew that way. Others were lighter because the artist favored bright colors. Because the series was divided into distinct storylines, it became the practice for one artist or artistic team to illustrate one story within the series itself. This gave each separate story an individual look. Only the cover artist, Dave McKean, remained a visual constant throughout the series.

The Sandman was a finite series, running from 1988 until 1996. The ongoing plot involved Dream engaging in a series of heroic tasks, following an archetypal hero's journey. Dream had to free himself from imprisonment and regain his kingdom. He had to win freedom for a lover who'd been tortured for ten thousand years. He had to find his own son, Orpheus, the musician from Greek mythology. Having completed his labors, he was then replaced by a new Sandman.

The Sandman enjoyed consistent and growing popularity among comic book readers for the first few years. Its multiple storylines containing elements of the horror genre and myriad cultural references satisfied many different kinds of readers. Gaiman's reputation in the comic book field was cemented by a string of other successes. Most notable of these, and the most accessible to nontraditional comic book readers, was *The Books of*

Magic series, the story of child who would grow into the greatest magician in the world.

In the early 1990s, *The Sandman's* popularity began to spread well beyond the comics field as favorable notices about the series appeared in the mainstream press. Gaiman was the subject of an article in *Rolling Stone,* and critic Frank McConnell compared *Sandman* favorably to James Joyce's *Ulysses* in *The Nation.* Other notices appeared, as well as sound bites from celebrities as diverse as Peter Straub, Roger Zelazny, and Norman Mailer. The

Morpheus (Neil Gaiman's *Sandman*) discusses his universal role with William Shakespeare in *The Tempest.*

series was awarded a World Fantasy award in 1991 for a story tracing Shakespeare's skills as a playwright back to a bargain he'd made with the Sandman, one of the few times a comic book story had been awarded such an honor. Riding on the series' success, DC Comics began to publish the monthly comic in book form. The first collection, A Doll's House, included a complete storyline. The second collection was a "best of" volume, containing unconnected stories and a sample comic book script, clearly aimed only at the comic book audience. And *The Sandman* did connect critically with the steady comic book readership. The series received eight Eisner Awards. These awards, named for Will Eisner, are awarded annually for excellence in the comic book field. This prompted further collections, and the complete series was published chronologically, as well as a related series of graphic novels featuring Dream's sister, Death. *The Sandman* was so successful as a series of graphic novels that it generated several ancillary books including: *The Sandman Companion, Sandman: The Dust Covers, The Quotable Sandman, The Sandman: Book of Dreams* (a collection of short prose stories about the Endless), *Sandman, King of Dreams,* and a short prose novel written by Gaiman himself and illustrated by Japanese artist Yoshitaka Amano, *The Sandman: The Dream Hunters.*

Gaiman's *Sandman* broke with the comic book formula in many ways, perhaps explaining its success with a nontraditional comic book readership. The character Sandman didn't appear on the cover of either the monthly comic book or the graphic novels. Instead, a cover was created that embodied the book's atmosphere. Much of fantasy literature's concern was the interaction of mortal lives with the supernatural, but the focal point of *The Sandman* was the ways supernatural forces interacted with humanity. This focus allowed the Endless to become characters who grew and changed, and as the broader storyline evolved, readers watched Dream find his own very human nature.

Gaiman's personality was also a factor is the book's success. Always approachable, and genuinely enjoying his success, Gaiman was a great interview, and a strong advocate for more literary comics. DC Comics made an unprecedented decision to end the series when he chose to leave the book. Gaiman deserves credit for breathing new life into genre stories and for his inventiveness in mixing elements in a way that pleased traditional readers and brought new readers to the comics field. Perhaps his most significant achievement, however, was in the quality of the themes and narratives of the works themselves. Gaiman realized that readers wanted to hear once again the story of why the supernatural would choose to interact with humanity. And through his writing, and his creative collaboration with the artists of the series, he was able to articulate the deeply resonant theme that even though the faces worn by humanity's most primal desires are only temporary, the desires themselves remain constant.

Here a great personal deed has room.
—Walt Whitman

Bone Wars
The Paradigm Shifts Into High Gear

One of the best examples of a little company holding its own on the same ground as the big companies is Cartoon Books. Started by cartoonist Jeff Smith and his wife Vijaya Iyer, the company published only one book, *Bone. Bone* had begun as a college newspaper strip, but Smith quickly realized he wasn't going to be able to tell the epic story he wanted to in the newspaper strip format. While working in animation, he became aware of the changing comic book industry, especially books like Maus and *Batman: The Dark Knight Returns.* He was impressed by the cinematic storytelling in *Dark Knight,* and the magnetic quality of *Maus,* while noting that both books had been packaged similarly to trade books. In 1991, he began publishing *Bone* as a black and white comic book fantasy, a story inspired by the work of Carl Barks, Walt Kelly's *Pogo, The Lord of the Rings, Star Wars, Moby Dick,* and Bugs Bunny cartoons. The comic book *Bone* was more fully formed than its newspaper strip predecessor. During the years since college, Smith had come to see *Bone* as a complete story. The plot featured the three Bone cousins lost in a pretechnological kingdom amid a brewing war between the forces of light and darkness.

The setup: Fone Bone searches for his cousins, Phoney and Smiley, after being swarmed by locusts in the first issue of *Bone*.

While the storytelling follows traditional mythic patterns, Smith created a lively narrative and a cast of engaging characters for *Bone*. The three Bone cousins are the heroes whose exploits, scrapes, and foibles propel the story: Fone, sensitive to the needs of others; Smiley, amoral and naïve; and Phoney, scheming and greedy, but always looking out for his cousins in a pinch. Also tossed into the mix is a teenage princess who doesn't know she's the heir to the kingdom's throne. The interplay between the four major characters was funny, and humor was a large part of the book's success, but drama and pathos were also evident. Another factor was the way the storytelling unfolded; the Bone cousins begin as observers, but as the war progresses they, like the reader, became participants. In some ways the most important key to *Bone's* success was Smith's remarkable talent as a storyteller, an artist and writer who could combine drawing, page design and narrative into a comic that completely engaged his readers. His no-nonsense storytelling techniques soon earned him widespread respect within the industry.

By 1993, *Bone* was considered to be a commercial and critical success, and Cartoon Books began collecting the comics into a graphic novel series. This decision caused waves in the comics community; back issues of the comic book series were considered valuable and sold at inflated prices. The buying and selling of rare comic books (the "collector's" market) was one of the economic realities of the comic book marketplace. Collecting a popular comic book series like *Bone* minimized the importance of buying back issues, and would cause the prices of back issues to drop. But the impulse behind the decision by Cartoon Books to collect the series was unrelated to the collecting of comics. It was done to keep the entire *Bone* series in print, exactly what any small publisher would do. Reprinting the books in this way made it easy for new readers to jump right into the story. It also encouraged readers uncomfortable with comic books to give the series a try. Clearly, Cartoon Books was on to something: the first of a projected nine graphic novels, *Bone: Out from Boneville,* sold 50,000 copies in eighteen months. It was also a personal milestone for Smith, who had wanted to produce a book-length cartoon since childhood. As he put it, "I wanted to create something in comics that up until that time I had only seen in prose: an epic on the scale of *War and Peace,* with a real beginning, middle, and end." Other companies might not have been so concerned with a beginning, middle and end, but they saw the sales figures. *Bone's* success with the graphic novel collections demonstrated the appeal and financial rewards of the format. Publishers small and large took notice, and the comic book field shifted even further than it had before to putting its products in book form.

Bone was promoted primarily by a combination of good reviews in the comic book field and by word of mouth among readers. The graphic novel series also helped Bone

The payoff: As usual, Fone finds Phoney and Smiley entrenched in yet another hair-brained scheme to get rich quick.

poke its head out of the comic book field but not, at first, because it found its way into bookstores. In the mid-1990s, *Bone* was embraced by the public library community. Not only did Bone's success move the comic book field further toward graphic novel publishing, its broad appeal helped open library shelves to works other than that new classic, Maus.

The success of *Bone* can be attributed to many factors; the comic book marketplace had evolved, and by studying it carefully, Cartoon Books was able to use the comic book marketplace to its advantage. Smith and Iyer made frequent appearances at comic book conventions and made personal contact with the comics retailers to help promote the *Bone* series.

One thing that both *Bone* and Neil Gaiman's *The Sandman* demonstrated was that a growing segment of the comic book readership had grown tired of superhero fantasy and was more interested in literary fantasy. Although very different, both books peaked around the same time in an expanding comic book marketplace, appealing to both male and female readers as well as readers outside comics. Both were perceived as original works, and their simultaneous success helped reinforce the changes that were happeneing in the comics field. All of these were important factors, but the primary reason for *Bone's* success was that Smith was able to express a personal vision while drawing on the conventions of fantasy literature and the familiar world of words and pictures storytelling.

Come my friends. 'Tis not too late to seek a newer world.
—Alfred Lord Tennyson

Understanding Comics
The Dream of a Common Language

Scott McCloud's breakthrough book, *Understanding Comics,* a 215-page exploration into how comics work and an explanation of what comics can be, was first published by Tundra/Kitchen Sink Press in 1993. Tundra was a small press started by Kevin Eastman, of *Teenage Mutant Ninja Turtles* fame. The idea behind Tundra was to support experiments using the comic book format, and many of these ventures weren't profitable. Kitchen Sink Press, a long-running and successful comic book publisher, merged with Tundra Publishing in 1992, so McCloud's book was one of the first books published by Tundra/Kitchen Sink Press.

Understanding Comics sprang fully grown on the reading public. Except for insiders, no one knew of its existence. No part of it appeared in serialized form prior to book-length publication. McCloud had been a comics professional for years, having worked briefly for DC Comics, but his most noteworthy achievement prior to *Understanding Comics* was an adventure series that he wrote and drew called *Zot!* This series used familiar comic book character types in a playful, direct way. As an artist and writer,

McCloud's work was defined by warmth, charm, and a lack of cynicism. *Zot!* served as a sort of counterpoint to the kind of postmodern superhero stories epitomized by Frank Miller's *Batman: The Dark Knight Returns, Zot!* was, in a way, a study in how superhero and adventure comics could work.

Observant readers weren't surprised when McCloud's *Understanding Comics* exhibited the same fresh traits first seen in *Zot!,* only this time around the focus wasn't on the telling of an adventure story but on the realm of comics itself. The book was partly an analysis of how comics were made, partly a history of comics, partly a study of how comics (or sequential art, storytelling pictures in sequence) worked, and mostly a wild, educational ride the likes of which readers inside and outside of comics had never seen before.

Low tech master villain Bellows suffers Zot's wrath … as it were. From the *Zot!* story, *Planet Earth.*

There was more to the book that just its application to comics. Many of McCloud's theories could be applied to other fields such as music and literature as well, thus giving readers outside of comics a comfortable point of reference. He also defined stages of artistic development as well as offering a very broad definition of what art is and the function it serves within society, all the while finding a way to make the comics medium the focal point of a wider discussion of the arts. His ideas were opinionated, controversial,

Scott McCloud's self-admittedly broad definition of "art," from *Understanding Comics*.

and invited discussion. It was McCloud's cheeky presentation, however, that really brought his theories to life. The character Scott McCloud (the "Understanding Comics" guy, as he called himself) appears dressed in glasses, sport jacket and wearing a T-shirt with a thunderbolt (a reference to *Zot!*), while the character Scott McCloud lectures the reader on comics history, comics theory and comics technique, the pages of the book around him are filled with visually arresting ploys that demonstrate his points. This quirky, vivid presentation caught readers' imaginations, and the first print run of *Understanding Comics* exceeded its initial expectation of 6,000 copies, selling 10,000 copies within the comics industry during the first month alone.

The book hit the mainstream shortly after its initial publication, garnering reviews in trade book publications such as *Publishers Weekly*, but the real noise was heard when it received high profile treatment in the *New York Times Book Review,* the *Boston Globe,* and the *Chicago Sun-Times.* McCloud became a symbol of the new, improved, comics field, and was frequently interviewed. In order to better educate book industry personnel to the potential of the comics medium, McCloud wrote and illustrated a lengthy article on comics that appeared in *Publishers Weekly.* The revolution that had begun with the publication of *Maus,* he warned, was going to be won, and publishing had better get ready for comics.

Now a decade old, *Understanding Comics* continues to sell steadily. McCloud has become a regular lecturer on the college circuit, and the book is frequently used in college courses. The success of *Understanding Comics* inspired McCloud to create a follow-up volume, *Reinventing Comics,* which focuses both on comics history and its potential as a Web-based medium. While *Reinventing Comics* was not as widely read as *Understanding Comics,* McCloud is one of the few breakthrough cartoonists who has produced a significant second work.

Understanding Comics was both a treatise and a shout: mainstream culture couldn't use ignorance as an excuse anymore. McCloud had given it the tools necessary to decode the confusing comics medium. The book was a form of exorcism and a turning point. Of *Understanding Comics,* McCloud said, "Having gratified my ego by producing something myself and others respect, in order to continue to be excited by this field, I need to set new goals for myself and define success differently in the future."

I think this is the beginning of a beautiful friendship.
—Humphrey Bogart, Casablanca

A Message in a Bottle
Notes From the Underground

In 1990, James Vance and Dan Burr's story of a boy's search for his father set against the backdrop of the Great Depression, *Kings in Disguise,* received a surprise award. *Publishers Weekly* named it one of the best paperbacks of 1990. This achievement indicated a more serious consideration of graphic novels by book industry publications. Even if *Kings in Disguise* rode on the coattails of *Maus* or *Watchmen,* in the sense that these books had primed the media to pay attention to quality graphic novels, it certainly stood on its own as a literary and artistic work. One could trace both *Maus* and *Watchmen* back to comic book roots. *Kings* seemed more like a serious novel with pictures than a long comic book. Published by Kitchen Sink Press, one of the first underground comix publishing houses, *Kings* represented a maturation of the underground comix movement; literary, well drawn, making a personal and political statement, and produced in black and white. The underground hadn't disappeared as its detractors had hoped. It had refined its art, waited until the comics' community was ready, and then proudly reared its head once again.

Signs of the underground revival had been seen within the comics field during the 1980s, when Fantagraphics Books published *Love & Rockets,* written and illustrated by brothers Gilbert and Jaime Hernandez. *Love & Rockets* told several stories simultaneously and mixed life in a rock band, life in a small Mexican town, and even a bit of science fiction. Complex, and involving several parallel storylines, it attracted a wide female readership and finally got noticed by *Rolling Stone* magazine in the early 1990s. Fantagraphics Books, the publisher, has since released the issues as a graphic novel series. Spiegelman's *Maus* was at its core a voice from the underground as well.

A typical scene of romantic struggle from Jaime Hernandez's seminal *Love & Rockets* story, *The Death of Speedy.*

A movement was afoot. Throughout the 1990s, black and white literary graphic novels were grabbing the attention of readers on both sides of the comic book store door. In 1992, Four Walls, Eight Windows released Eric Drooker's scratchboard picture novel, *Flood!* The book told a chilling, surrealistic, wordless urban story. An artist is laid off from his job and then has a brief affair with a junkie. Afterward, he returns to his loft to create the book *Flood!* which the reader holds. Drooker had been influenced by the German Expressionists and Fran Masereel's wordless picture novels *Passionate Journey* and *The City.* More contemporary influences were Robert Crumb, Art Spiegelman, and Will Eisner. Produced over a five-year period, artist Drooker considered *Flood!* to be a vast personal statement.

The book was difficult to define. It looked more like an art book than anything that might spring from within the comics industry. However, the effect was hypnotic. It was a Zen experience; if you liked *Flood!,* you got it, if you didn't really get it you didn't care for it. The book received notices in major media outlets, was short-listed for the National Book Award, and was given an American Book Award. However, at the time, few either outside or inside the comic book field saw Flood! as an example of the evolving graphic novel form.

The scratchboard art style that was so effective in *Flood!* again attracted readers beyond the comic book marketplace when NBM published Peter Kuper's lively book, *Give It Up! and Other Stories by Franz Kafka.* Classic story adaptation was a staple of the comic book industry, an avenue explored thoroughly by NBM publishing. The company had released many comic book versions of children's books which had found their way outside the comic book field, notably P. Craig Russell's bright, cartoony, *Fairy Tales of Oscar Wilde* series. However, in this version, Kuper hadn't only made Kafka available to new readers, he'd interpreted the stories. The black and white art might have been worth thousands of words, but it didn't make comprehending the Kafka stories easier.

Kuper had been working on both sides of the comic book field for years. At first, he was powerfully influenced by the work of Jack Kirby, and he continued to draw on the fluidity and movement of Kirby's comic book pages as he added more meaningful elements to his artistic repertoire. He became the co-editor of a political anthology comic book, *World War III Illustrated,* and was the only cartoonist to have a regular comic strip appearing in the *New York Times.* He chose to interpret Kafka because "the work spoke to me and transcended the time that it was made." Working on the book in his spare time, *Give It Up!* took him eight years to produce, but it was time well spent, because, according to Kuper, interpreting Kafka's work "freed up my storytelling." In 1995, Kuper was named comic book artist of the year by *Rolling Stone* magazine.

Give It Up! received special notice on National Public Radio and in the *New York Times.* General readers were drawn to it, possibly because it looked so unlike a comic

Peter Kuper's graphic depiction of Franz Kafka's *Fratricide,* from *Give it Up!*

A frank opinion from Joe Sacco's *Palestine*.

book and because Kafka's work continued to fascinate mainstream readers. The book remains the only adult interpretation of a literary work to be embraced outside of the comic book field. Some graphic novels that made it out of the comic book world did so in part because they didn't remind trade book readers of comic books.

Readers were given yet another example of the potential of the graphic novel when Fantagraphics Books published Joe Sacco's *Palestine* in 1996. A self-described comics journalist, Sacco's artistic style had been heavily influenced by underground comix legend Robert Crumb. Sacco mixed his personality into the journalistic process, perhaps influenced both by Crumb's autobiographical cartooning and the personal reporting of New Journalism. Whereas a media journalist might have days or weeks to research and report a story, Sacco spent months interviewing his subjects and getting to know them and what their lives were like. As a result, *Palestine* attempted to tell the human story behind the Middle Eastern conflict. Washed with a brown glow, *Palestine* made a small bang this side of the comic book field, chiefly because of the topic, and walked away with an American Book Award.

Meanwhile, in the wider entertainment and educational communities, supporters of the graphic novel—novelists, movie directors, magazine editors, booksellers, librarians and academics—all began exploring the uses of this newly-prominent form. The comic book industry had been the subject of serious novels as far back as 1977, when Robert Meyer wrote *Super-Folks,* a book using cultural heroes such as Batman, Superman, and John F. Kennedy as focal points. Tom De Haven's trilogy about the comic book industry began in 1985, with the publication of *Funny Papers,* set in the 1890s against the backdrop of the germinating comic strip. De Haven followed with *Derby Dugan's Depression Funnies.* The second novel was placed in the 1930s and used the heyday of the adventure comic strip as its focus. The trilogy concluded in 2001, when De Haven published *Dugan Underground,* which delved into the underground comix movement and counterculture of the 1960s.

In 1988, Jay Cantor, already well regarded as a fiction experimentalist, published his "novel in five panels," *Krazy Kat.* Where De Haven had used the comic book field as history, and Meyer had hoed its fertile ground for symbolism, Cantor gave literary life to Herriman's comic strip characters. Observant readers were learning that serious novelists respected the comic book field.

Fictional work focusing on the comic book industry continued. In 1993, Steven

Millhauser published his gem of a novella, *The Little Kingdom of J. Franklin Payne,* in which cartoonist Payne is gradually pulled deeper and deeper into a fantasy world that he created. 1994 brought Robert Rodi's *What They Did to Princess Paragon,* a novel that explored the current comic book field, focusing on the world of the comic book convention.

But the biggest boost the comics field received from the literary world came from Michael Chabon's novel, *The Amazing Adventures of Kavalier and Clay,* published in 2000. A highly respected novelist whose novel *Wonder Boys* had been made into a movie with big name stars, Chabon used the comic book industry of the 1930s as a backdrop to tell a story about artists, immigrants, families, financial success, and repressed lives. The plot came to a crucial climax during the Senate hearings of the 1950s when the comic book industry had almost been destroyed. Finally, someone had told fiction readers what had happened inside the comic book industry. Readers and critics listened: *The Amazing Adventures of Kavalier and Clay* was awarded a Pulitzer Prize.

Chabon's *Kavalier & Clay*, with its faked distressed edges and all.

In addition to novelists, movie directors were drawing upon the comic book world as well. In 1995, director Terry Zwigoff released *Crumb,* a biting biographical study of underground cartoonist Robert Crumb, and Kevin Smith used the world of alternative comics as the background for his 1996 film about confused relationships, *Chasing Amy.*

While novelists and movie directors were looking to comic books for inspiration, magazine writers who had grown up reading comics were turning to the growing number of graphic novels as material for reviews and articles. Throughout the 1990s, publications aimed at the trade book and library fields—most notably *Publishers Weekly* and *Booklist*—reviewed graphic novels and offered information to interested professionals about the changing comics industry. Toward the end of the 1990s, public librarians embraced the graphic novel medium, their interest fueled by the readabability of graphic novels and the high quality of some of these books. Among bookstore personnel, people who had grown up reading comics and watching the field mature began to have an impact on the business. As a result, many chain and independent bookstores included graphic novel sections, generally as part of their humor or fantasy/science fiction sections. Throughout the 1990s, several trade publishing houses began experimenting with their own graphic novel lines, hoping to duplicate the success that Pantheon had had with *Maus.* Most of these experiments were short lived because there were not all that many graphic novels that genuinely appealed to mainstream audiences. Only driven cartoonists such as Drooker, Kuper, or Spiegelman were willing to put years into a personal project not knowing whether or not the book would move beyond or even sell to the comic book readership. Most preferred

The teen angst of Rebecca and Enid from Dan Clowes's *Ghost World.*

the steady paycheck that smart and appealing genre work offered.

Academia was also showing an interest in the growing comics field, and courses on comics as art and literature could be found sprinkled across the country. The University of Mississippi Press had its own imprint about comics, launched under the guidance of Faulkner specialist and comics historian M. Thomas Inge. Outside professional journals, in the more accessible world of mainstream journalism, sporadic articles about comics and graphic novels appeared in newspapers and hip magazines across the United States. The irregularity of these articles irritated some within the comics field, but there was no denying that the general public was getting more frequent information about what was happening in comics than before. Again, Art Spiegelman was highly visible, but this time as a cover artist for the *New Yorker.* He also wrote articles on comics creators for the *New Yorker* and brought other cartoonists to the magazine to do covers and illustrations.

Meanwhile, back inside the blossoming comic book and graphic novel industry, Fantagraphics Books scored a major mainstream hit with Dan Clowes's tale of teenage angst, *Ghost World,* in 1997. Perfect in tone and presentation, *Ghost World* dissected deteriorating teen friendships as the characters began the process of moving toward adult maturity. Beautifully illustrated in soft colors, *Ghost World's* resolution packed the kind of knockout punch that readers expected from a novel about youthful restlessness. In contrast to the work produced by Drooker and Sacco, *Ghost World* felt more like a comic book, perhaps because of the subject matter. There was no denying that in Clowes's hands cartooning was a perfected instrument.

The book received some media notice, but its success relied as much on proselytizing by devoted readers. On both sides of the cultural divide *Ghost World* enthusiasts grabbed friends by their shirt collars and pulled them into corners, telling them in no uncertain terms that if they didn't pick up *Ghost World,* they would never speak to them again.

While these changes originating from the comic book industry were happening, the career of strip cartoonist Ben Katchor was taking off. Katchor had been publishing strips in alternative papers since 1988. His work could be characterized as very theatrical, and his strips created a haunting memory of a city like his native New York, but a city that never was. His primary character was Julius Knipl, real estate photographer, and as Knipl views the city through his lens, Katchor presents a portrait of an urban community through his character. Because he'd created a pseudofantasy, he was free to use whatever material found its way into his stories, and Jewish culture saturated the Julius Knipl stories. Katchor's work was collected into four volumes. After his first collection, Katchor moved to Pantheon Books, the publisher of *Maus.* Pantheon was looking for comic properties that would have the same kind of broad appeal as *Maus,* books in comic format that would appeal to non-comics readers. The experiment worked: many of Katchor's readers are not committed to the comics format, and read no other cartoonist but Ben Katchor. The cartoon format appealed to Katchor because "it covered the full spectrum of meaning: image can give concrete ideas to text." In addition, Katchor considered the comics format to be a version of the theatre translated to the drawn and printed page. His influences ranged from the stylized works of Edward Gorey and Saul Steinberg to the solid and believeable figure work of *Spider-Man* artist Steve Ditko. In recognition of his incisive cartooning, Katchor was awarded a Guggenheim in 1996 and in 2000, a MacArthur Fellowship, commonly known as the genius award. On the other side of the Atlantic, master cartoonist Raymond Briggs created a graphic novel of his own, Ethel and Ernest, a memoir of his parents' lives.

In 2000, the graphic novel took another giant leap forward: Pantheon Books, the graphic novel's most ardent supporter in the trade publishing field, published three books, two of which came from the Fantagraphics line-up: Dan Clowes's *David Boring,* and *Jimmy Corrigan: The Smartest Kid on Earth,* by cartoonist newcomer to the mainstream, Chris Ware. Clowes returned to familiar ground with *David Boring,* the story of a nineteen-year-old security guard who finds, then loses, and then finds again the perfect woman. Readers were, however, unprepared for Chris Ware's masterpiece, *Jimmy Corrigan: The Smartest Kid on Earth.* Jimmy Corrigan is no longer a kid but an adult who has suffered for a lifetime under a domineering mother. Through a series of unexpected events, Jimmy learns the identity of his father, who is recovering from a car accident. While at the hospital, Jimmy meets his half sister and begins the slow, difficult journey toward adulthood. The narrative of this graphic novel was unusual, even in the diverse group of works that had captured attention beyond comics, but that was only half of *Jimmy Corrigan.* The other half was the presentation. Challenging the reader to pay full attention, the panels didn't always flow in a logical pattern. Ware was using the comics format to purposely disorient the

One of several generations of Jimmy Corrigans from Chris Ware's *Jimmy Corrigan: The Smartest Kid on Earth.*

reader, in an attempt to have the reader experience Corrigan's view of the world. Ware's book also used more color than other graphic novels embraced by mainstream culture. Meticulously drawn and referencing classic painters, another caveat was that *Jimmy Corrigan* was like a book-length M. C. Escher print: the more you looked, the more there was to see. *Jimmy Corrigan* was awarded the Guardian Prize in 2001, the only graphic novel to earn such an honor.

The publicity wheels available to Pantheon Books were rolling, and all three books received major notices including reviews in the *New York Times.* The publisher also sent the creators on a national bookstore signing tour unprecedented for cartoonists.

The graphic novel, a cartoon literary art form, had arrived. The impulse that had originated with underground comix and had been modified by the mainstream comics industry, had moved outside the comics field into the wider world. Combined influences from inside and outside the comics field had propelled this new form to forefront of popular culture. People who had come of age since the comics field began to view itself as a serious art form were now deciding the direction of the culture itself.

"Pinch me, I must be dreaming,"--Larry Fine, the Three Stooges

A New Millennium For Comics

As we entered the new millennium, public interest in graphic novels increased. In 2002 the first Spider-man movie appeared, with a big name cast and a bigger budget. The well done movie performed exceedingly well at the box office. Spider-man's sequel, co-written by Michael Chabon, also performed well, ushering in an era of movies featuring the Marvel superheroes. Although these movies had little to do with the heroes appearing in comic books and graphic novels, feature films made these characters instantly recognizable to the world outside comics. Superhero stories proved to be an effective metaphor for the post 9-11 world; from 2002-2011, 47 superhero movies appeared in theaters, with more in production. The success of superhero films gave way to film adaptations of more serious graphic novels such as Harvey Pekar's *American Splendor* (2003) starring Paul Giamatti and Hope Davis. Film companies discovered that, as a general rule, movies based on graphic novels grossed more money than films based on other kinds of stories, partially because the graphic novel format lent itself handily to movie

American Splendor: Ego & Hubris by Pekar & Dumm

adaptation. As a result, graphic novel based movies paraded through theaters from 2002 onward whether or not the movie goers were familiar with the graphic novel upon which the movies were based.

2002 was a turning point for the graphic novel industry in another way as well; the American Library Association held a day long symposium on graphic novels in libraries at their annual meeting. Speakers included cartoonists Art Spiegelman, Jeff Smith, Neil Gaiman, Colleen Doran, and librarian Stephen Weiner. Several other librarians also spoke, extolling the virtues of adding graphic novels to library collections. This conference and others, especially the graphic novel program sponsored earlier that same year at the annual meeting of the Public Library Association, indicated continued institutional interest in using and studying graphic novels.

All this promotion of the graphic novel fueled more interest in the form from major publishing houses, and those who didn't have graphic novel imprints developed them. Scholastic, flush with the success of the *Harry Potter* series, initiated their own graphic novel line, *Graphix*, by presenting a colorized version of Jeff Smith's series *Bone*. This

Jeff Smith's *Bone* enjoyed a second life in color from Scholastic's *Graphix* line.

effort was successful; between 2005 and 2010, Scholastic sold several million copies of *Bone*. Scholastic's success emboldened other children's publishers to emulate *Bone's* success with varying results. Even more commercially successful than *Bone* was Jeff Kinney's half-graphic novel series, *The Diary of a Wimpy Kid* (2007--). Originally an online comic, *The Wimpy Kid* gave way to many sequels and a movie franchise. *The Wimpy Kid* became a publishing phenomenon, with print runs in the millions, and spawned many imitators. Graphic novel imprints coming out from trade houses helped promote graphic novels published by small publishers as well, although it wasn't unusual for a trade house to republish a graphic novel for a wider audience after the small publisher had taken the initial risk and found a hit book.

Manga, which had been growing in popularity in the 1990s, reached new heights by late 2004. Part of the appeal of Manga was that almost every conceivable kind of story

Dynamic and exotic (read from right to left), *Naruto* by Masashi Kishimoto.

was told. Other components were the standardized, cartoony, drawing style and a growing interest in Japanese culture. Still another part was the "book" effect. Because American readers saw so little Manga serialized, it appeared primarily in "graphic novel" form, and for an affordable price. Among the most popular of the Manga books were *Naruto, Fruit Baskets, Chobits* and *Death Note*. These books appealed primarily to teenagers but adults were drawn to them as well. While it rose steadily from 2002-2007, the popularity of the Manga form began to wane in 2008, although it remained a strong piece of the graphic novel market, promoted by its counterpart, Japanese animation, called Anime.

Canadian cartoonists were making a big impact on American readers. Seth, whose early books included the autobiographical tale, *It's a Good Life if You Don't Weaken* (1996) produced well received graphic novels such as *Clyde Fans* (2000-2004) about a family fan business unable to adapt to air conditioning and *Wimbledon Green* (2005) about the world's greatest comic book collector and newcomer Jeff Lemire broke out with his book, *The Complete Essex County* (2007-2010) illuminating life in rural Canada, which centered around family secrets, the landscape, and ice hockey.

The first volume of many in the complete reprint of *Peanuts*.

Classic comic strips were-presented in new, attractive packaging, exemplified by Fantagraphics Books republishing of Charles Schulz's classic strip, *The Complete Peanuts*, beginning in 2004. The hardcover editions were pleasing and had an archival sensibility. Readers responded, and *The Complete Peanuts* spent significant time on The New York Times Best Seller list. Fantagraphics Books followed with *The Complete Dennis the Menace*, and *The Complete Pogo*. Other companies followed suit, especially IDW with the *Library of American Comics,* and it became common to find many older comic strips reprinted in attractive, affordable editions.

International literary graphic novels flourished. Leading the way was Marjane Satrapi's autobiographical book about growing up in Iran, *Persepolis* (2003). The sequel, *Persepolis 2* appeared in 2004 and the movie version in 2007. As *Maus*, had done, Persepolis cemented the position of the adult autobiographical graphic novel.

Prominent fictional American graphic novels for adults found increasingly receptive audiences, among them Craig Thompson's *Blankets* (2003) about a boy growing up in a religious household, and Charles Burn's *Black Hole* (2005) about some teens shunned by society after developing an AIDS like disease. Perhaps the best recognized of these books

Alison vs. Dad in Bechdel's autobiographical *Fun Home*.

was Alison Bechdel's autobiographical book, *Fun Home: a family tragicomic* (2006) about a young woman trying to resolve her gay father's suicide. Fun Home was awarded the Los Angeles Times' Book of the Year.

As the decade drew to a close, the grandmaster of alternative comics returned with a respectful, incisive, humanistic examination of the first book of the bible in *The Book of Genesis*, Illustrated by R. Crumb (2009) which landed on best seller lists as well as receiving critical accolades. During the new millennium, not only had mainstream readers begun to appreciate graphic novels, they had learned to respect them as well.

"Why don't we live here?"--Bill Murray, Groundhog Day

What's Next for Graphic Novels?

The future for the graphic novel looks even more promising as we move through the second decade of the new millennium. Support from institutions outside of comic book publishers will allow for an even greater variety of graphic novels to be produced. This will draw a larger reader base to the comics' form. Continued media coverage as well as Hollywood's fondness for the graphic novel continues to bring the form increased visibility.

Trade publishers' imprints will insure that graphic novels have more outlets than in previous years; however that change has necessitated that more mainstream stories be told. While that has allowed the form to develop artistically on one level, for the most part the adult imprints are fairly conservative, and focus on autobiographies and nonfiction.

Children's imprints almost ignored the autobiographical genre altogether, and instead produced a healthy dose of fantasy stories, humor, and nonfiction. There is presently an explosion in kids comics, the fastest growing segment, involving many estab-

A multimedia darling from comics: *Walking Dead* by Robert Kirkman.

lished children's publishers successfully doing biographies, history and adaptations of classics, besides adapting famous licensed properties.

However, graphic novels published by comic book publishers remain critical because these books are the major testing ground for trade publishers. As we go forward, trade houses will need to develop methods of attracting top flight cartoonists independently from observing successful efforts produced by comic book publishers and then offering these cartoonists large enough advances to lure them away from smaller companies. This talent scouting method strains both the trade houses and comic book publishers. Because trade houses produce books aimed at general audiences, one drawback of their interest is the minimization of what Frank Miller has called the "outsider" status of the cartoonist. The danger of alienating the "outsider" position is that this is the reservoir where many of the best cartoonists draw creative sustenance. Those books emerging from the "outsider" position will most likely be published by comic book publishers as opposed to trade houses.

Self-publishing has been an important part of the comic book marketplace since the early 1980s. Self and small publishing houses will remain essential in bringing out new voices whether or not these voices reach the mainstream readership directly. For a springboard, besides online comics, there is a growing phenomemon in crowd sourced funding, especially on the site Kickstarter which, as of this writing, has suddenly become a de-facto leading "publisher."

Graphic novels will keep pace with technological developments in the publishing industry. The large comic book publishers currently release paper and e-issues simultaneously and at the same price. This practice demonstrates that currently the readership is split fairly between paper and electronic formats. There's a physical component to the comics' format. Readers often want to hold the periodical after reading the same issue electronically. However, many young people began reading after graphic novels became popular, so, as this segment of the readership grows, comic books may become a specialty item.

The comic book store will survive, ironically aided by trade publishers and graphic novel sections at chain bookstores and public libraries. The wide focus on graphic novels continues to build a bigger readership, and no bookstore carries as diverse collection as a credible comic book store. Purchasing from online book sellers may prove to be inexpensive, but online resources minimize the browsing aspect of book selection. It remains essential that committed graphic novel readers have access to a comic book store.

Trends come and begin to go. The Manga craze demonstrated how one segment of the industry may dominate sales for many years and then wane. Right now, we're experiencing a "French invasion" in terms of adult graphic novels, similar to the way popular music experienced a "British invasion" in the 1960s. Earlier, we experienced a Manga "invasion". Interest in international graphic novels will fuel more foreign "invasions" in coming years as we learn more about the graphic novels produced in other countries.

Finally, a word needs to be said about the wide array of opportunities offered cartoonists in the coming years. Now that American readers have accepted stories told in cartoon format, widespread support of this form from various segments of our culture has created a fertile ground for established and budding cartoonists to tell the stories that they want to and are skilled enough to accomplish, allowing readers to discover and rediscover themselves in the newest evolution of the comic art form—the graphic novel.

French invasion: absurdist humor from *Salvatore* by De Crécy.

Every man's work, whether it be literature or music or pictures or architecture or anything else, is always a portrait of himself, and the more he tries to conceal himself the more clearly will his character appear in spite of him.

—Samuel Butler

Further Reading

Most of the graphic novels discussed throughout this book are in print, and may be found by doing an author/title search. Many of the books are now published by a second or third publisher. Your public library is a good place to start looking for these books. This bibliography includes a range of recommended books about the comics field.

Eisner, Will
Graphic Storytelling and Visual Narrative (Will Eisner Instructional Books)
W.W. Norton, 2008
Master cartoonist Eisner examines cartooning skills such as lettering, shading, importance of representational objects, and layouts. A valuable tool for aspiring cartoonists.

Feiffer, Jules
The Great Comic Book Heroes
Fantagraphics Books, 2003
Feiffer's seminal 1965 essay is now back in print. Part an ode to the early days of the comic book industry, part social commentary, and part memoir, this work ignited comics fans in the 1960s.

Hadju, David
The Ten-Cent Plague: The Great Comic-Book Scare and How It Changed America
Picador; First Edition, 2009
Hadju ably studies the comics industry in the 1940s and 50s, and relies on personal narrative, worldly events, and the censorship battles led by Frederic Wertham which almost shut down the comic book industry. Well researched, this book reveals the way the American comics industry was stopped in its tracks in the 1950s, only to recover in the 1990s.

Jones, Gerard
Men of Tomorrow: Geeks, Gangsters, and the Birth of the Comic Book
Basic Books, 2005
Jones studies the early days of the comic book industry, which included mob connections as well as extremely poor working conditions. He focuses on Jerry Siegel and Joe Shuster, the co-creators of Superman, and explores their rise and fall in the comic book world.

Kidd, Chip
Shazam! The Golden Age of the World's Mightiest Mortal
Abrams ComicArts , 2010
Captain Marvel and his family (Mary Marvel, Captain Marvel Jr., etc) were extremely popular heroes in the 1940s and 50s, until the Marvel franchise was stopped cold by DC Comics. This book is a tribute to Captain Marvel, and contains all the visual innovation and goofiness that made the character popular.

Levitz, Paul
75 Years of DC Comics: The Art of Modern Mythmaking
Taschen; 2nd edition 2010
Epic in scope, this book weighs in at a whopping 720 pages. Levitz, former President of DC Comics, chronicles both the characters DC has offered over the years and the creators the company has employed. Well known cartoonists are studied as well as lesser known creators. A masterwork of comics' history.

Sabin, Roger
Comics, Comix & Graphic Novels: A History of Comic Art
Phaidon, 2001
This history of comics is well researched and presented. He traces the history of comics from the 12th century to contemporary graphic novels, while including well chosen illustrations. This book offers an excellent overview of the comics field.

Witek, Joseph
Comic Books as History: The Narrative Art of Jack Jackson, Art Spiegelman, and Harvey Pekar
University Press of Mississippi, 1990
Witek uses critical methodology while examining the work of current cartoonists. This is a particularly useful work as it includes a lengthy study of Spiegelman's *Maus.*

Wright, Bradford
Comic Book Nation: The Transformation of Youth Culture In America
John Hopkins University Press, 2001
Wright offers a lively, well documented history of the mainstream comics industry. Insightfully, he places the comic book industry within the wider canvas of American history.

Other books by Stephen Weiner

The Will Eisner Companion
with N.C. Christopher Couch

101 Best Graphic Novels

100 Graphic Novels for Public Libraries

Bring an Author to Your Library

Hellboy: The Companion
with Jason Hall and Victoria Blake

Using Graphic Novels in the Classroom: A Guide For Teachers and Librarians

Critical Survey of Graphic Novels

NBM has over 200 graphic novels from America and Europe available.
Ask for our complete color catalog:
NBM Publishing
160 Broadway, Suite 700, East Wing,
New York, NY 10038

Visit our Web site to view our complete catalog and order any of our publications.
Librarians: visit our Library page at our Web site for recommendations
www.nbmpublishing.com

Stephen Weiner is director of the Maynard Public Library, in Maynard, Massachusetts, and a comics historian and critic who has been a pioneering advocate for graphic novels in public libraries and education. He has been writing about comic art since 1992, and has published numerous articles and reviews in magazines including *Library Journal, School Library Journal,* the *Voice of Youth Advocates,* and the *Shy Librarian.* He holds a master's degree in children's literature from Simmons College and a M.L.I.S. from the University of Rhode Island. In addition to his previous books on comic art, *100 Graphic Novels for Public Libraries* (Kitchen Sink Press) and *The 101 Best Graphic Novels* (NBM), he is also the author of *Bring an Author to Your Library* (The Highsmith Press), co-author with N. C. Christopher Couch of *The Will Eisner Companion* (DC Comics), author of *Hellboy: the Companion* (with Jason Hall and Victoria Blake) and *Using Graphic Novels in the Classroom: A Guide for Teachers and Librarians.* He has contributed to many anthologies and is co-editor of the encyclopedia series: *Critical Survey of Graphic Novels* (Salem Press).

Illustration by Chris Shadoian